The Complex PTSD Journal

The COMPLEX PTSD Journal

A Guided Journal to Help You Heal, Grow, and Thrive

Mercedes J. Okosi, PsyD

ROCKRIDGE
PRESS

This Journal Belongs To:

_____

Introduction

Welcome to *The Complex PTSD Journal: A Guided Journal to Help You Heal, Grow, and Thrive.* I am Dr. Mercedes J. Okosi, a licensed clinical psychologist in New York City and a specialist in trauma and post-traumatic stress disorder (PTSD). I have treated people of all ages with all sorts of traumas, including those related to chronic childhood abuse and neglect, community violence, natural disasters, sexual abuse and assault, and war. I have seen my patients heal and grow through actively confronting their trauma symptoms.

You have likely picked up this journal because symptoms related to your complex trauma continue to be distressing. My hope is that the tools and practices within these pages will assist you on your journey to healing.

Though trauma reactions are intense, they are to be expected in the face of unexpected threatening circumstances. That you would experience a range of complicated and difficult emotions in response to terrible traumatic events makes sense. Complex post-traumatic stress disorder (C-PTSD) is a reaction to prolonged or chronic traumatic events that encompasses not only the classic symptoms of PTSD but also additional symptoms that include dissociation and that impact mood regulation. Psychiatrist and educator Judith Lewis Herman was the first, in 1992, to propose that this mental health condition be viewed as a diagnosis separate from PTSD. And in 2018, C-PTSD was recognized in the World Health Organization's *International Classification of Diseases* (ICD-11). However, the *Diagnostic and Statistical Manual of Mental Disorders* (DSM-5), an additional standard diagnostic reference text for mental health professionals, does not yet recognize this distinction from the standard diagnosis of PTSD. The DSM-5 does acknowledge, however, that some people who have experienced trauma may display depressive, aggressive, or dissociative features in addition to anxiety and fear. Whereas new evidence continues to emerge, certain interventions tailored to distinct presentations of people's experiences of post-trauma are critical in offering help.

Individuals who have experienced prolonged chronic traumas, especially during their early development, will often exhibit the symptoms of PTSD including reexperiencing the trauma, avoiding reminders, having negative thoughts and moods, and living with hyperarousal and hypervigilance. According to research conducted by clinical psychologist Andreas Maercker and colleagues in 2013, people with C-PTSD are likely to also experience a particular symptom profile that includes deep shame or guilt, dissociation, emotional numbness, feelings of worthlessness, and difficulty being close with others. Several studies have found these symptoms in people who have lived with traumatic events like chronic child abuse, combat, community violence, family violence, neglect, sexual abuse, or acts of terrorism. This journal is not meant for self-diagnosis, but the tools offered here may help you manage your unique experiences.

This journal is also *not* a substitute for professional mental health services. However, journaling can help you get started with your recovery or can supplement therapy sessions. The prompts, practices, and affirmations in this journal are aimed at managing emotions, practicing coping skills, and establishing healthier relationships, including your relationship with yourself.

Use this journal as a safe space to process and reflect on your complex trauma experiences. My hope is that despite the great difficulties you face, you will gain resilience and begin healing with this journal's guidance.

How to Use This Journal

The *Complex PTSD Journal* consists of four sections that address major areas of your life that are impacted by trauma and require attention in the recovery process. These sections are arranged loosely chronologically—the past (section 1), present (sections 2 and 3), and future (section 4)— in terms of focus on the healing process. However, utilizing the sections out of chronological order depending on what is salient for you in the moment is fine as well. Specifically, "Section 1: Healing Wounds of the Past" helps you recognize the impact of trauma in the context of your life and begin to develop a basic sense of safety from which to move on to learn more skills. "Section 2: Exploring the Mind-Body Connection" provides suggestions to explore and manage the ways that chronic trauma has impacted you as a whole person so that you may reestablish a balanced connection between thoughts, emotions, and bodily sensations. "Section 3: Cultivating a Healthy Sense of Self" guides you toward compassion and care for your needs, desires, and boundaries, a critical part of healing. "Section 4: Continuing Your Healing Journey" focuses on the possibilities for growth and resilience after complex trauma.

Each of the four sections contains 20 prompts aimed at inspiring you to reflect, write, or act (or any combination of the three) toward gaining insight and a positive outlook. The five practices in each section are actionable skills you can use to directly address symptoms and distress. The five affirmations in each section are inspiring and positive phrases that can help shift your perspective or lift your mood. I encourage you to revisit these uplifting words as often as is helpful and to choose some to become regular parts of your healing process. You might copy them onto note cards to display around your home.

There is no right or wrong way to use this journal. You can work through the sections from start to finish or jump to the sections that seem most pressing to you. You may go through the prompts, practices, and affirmations as part of your daily routine, discover favorites to hold on to, or turn to this guidebook specifically when you encounter distress. The goal is to help you feel more equipped to manage your symptoms and experiences in a way that feels sustainable for your life.

Please be mindful that this journal is not a replacement for professional psychotherapy, medication management, or other professional mental health or medical services. Seeking out professional help is one of the most compassionate things you can do for yourself if symptoms begin to significantly impact your functioning. Please seek professional care if experiences of anxiety, depression, or hopelessness become unmanageable.

Recovering from trauma and C-PTSD will mean both building on the strengths you already possess and being open to developing a tool kit of new skills you can carry with you for life. The great news is that it is never too late to start this process.

Healing Wounds of the Past

One of the most fundamental aspects of healing and recovering from chronic traumatic experiences is establishing a sense of safety. For some, doing so may mean reestablishing a state of safety and balance that had been previously experienced but disturbed by trauma. For others, establishing a sense of safety may be an entirely new endeavor that they are trying for the first time. Traumatic experiences, especially those that are prolonged and compounded, can be extremely disruptive to our basic needs for safety, trust, and predictability.

Often, chaotic environments do not cultivate opportunities to get these needs met or to learn self-reliance to fulfill these critical needs. Complex trauma dramatically shifts our view of how we see and experience ourselves, others, and the world. Fortunately, we have a considerable capacity to find safety again and explore new possibilities in our lives.

Of course, important work is not always easy. Having fears and hesitations about the memories and feelings that will inevitably arise when confronting trauma head-on is normal. There may be frustrations and setbacks as you cope with symptoms. However, the increased sense of control and freedom you can gain will be worth the effort.

Life-altering experiences can be incredibly transformative. During your walk down the winding path of healing from complex trauma, there are also opportunities to find meaning, make new connections, and grow even more resilient. Indeed, part of healing from trauma is gaining an understanding of the whole scope of your life, including difficult experiences, and reimagining a way forward. These tools can be the first steps on that path.

The following activities will help you look at where you stand now in terms of your knowledge about C-PTSD, your current symptoms and stressors impacting your life, your goals, and your motivations to change. You'll begin to practice some baseline coping skills to carry with you throughout this process. In order to plan your recovery, you must first understand where you have been as well as where you are now.

Take a moment to write down how you imagine your life looking and feeling with few or no complex trauma-related symptoms. In this imagined life: How do you feel about yourself? What activities make you feel fulfilled? What kinds of people are part of your life?

I have many personal strengths that will allow me to achieve my goals.

Reflect on your existing strengths that will help you in your healing and list them. How did you develop these strengths and in what other scenarios have you used them?

_____

_____

_____

_____

_____

_____

_____

_____

_____

_____

_____

_____

_____

_____

_____

_____

_____

GOALS, MOTIVATION, AND BARRIERS

Actively tracking your level of motivation and being prepared to tackle barriers is critical to achieving goals.

1. Think about some specific goals you would like to achieve in your life. Perhaps you have goals related to school, work, interpersonal relationships, self-esteem, or specific trauma symptoms. List them below.

_____

_____

_____

_____

_____

_____

_____

_____

_____

_____

_____

_____

_____

_____

_____

_____

_____

_____

2. Rate your current level of motivation for each goal using the ruler below.

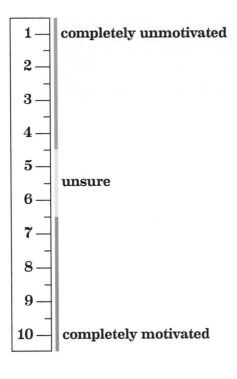

3. Consider your motivation scores and ask yourself, "Why isn't my score lower?" For example, if you record a 4, ask what made you choose the 4 and not a 2 or 3?

_____

_____

_____

4. Write down some of the reasons you're motivated to achieve these goals.

_____

_____

_____

_____

_____

5. What barriers, including complex trauma symptoms, may be getting in the way of achieving these goals?

_____

_____

_____

_____

_____

My trauma experiences do not define me. I am capable of creating safety and balance in my life.

Tell at least one person you feel safe with and trust that you are starting or continuing this healing process. How did that (those) conversation(s) go?

What did you know about C-PTSD before picking up this journal? Where did you get this information? What more have you learned so far? What more are you hoping to learn?

Think about areas of your life impacted by trauma. Consider, for example, friendships, romantic or sexual relationships, school, work, or any area appropriate to your situation. Which areas are impacted most and which are least impacted? What helps you manage areas in which you are doing well? What actions can you take to improve the other areas?

TRAUMA MYTHS

Read the list of statements below and mark them as either true or false. (See answers and more information on page 14.)

1. _____ The best way to deal with trauma is to avoid thoughts and feelings about it.

2. _____ The physical health of people who have experienced complex trauma, especially during childhood, may be impacted.

3. _____ If my therapist doesn't ask about trauma, I shouldn't bring up my experience.

4. _____ Many people can successfully recover from C-PTSD.

5. _____ Only violent, near-death experiences are considered traumas.

ANSWERS:

1. **False.** In 2012, Badour et al. found that avoidance made trauma symptoms worse in an adult sample and Shenk et al. studied the phenomenon of experiential avoidance facilitating the development of PTSD in survivors of childhood abuse. Avoidance is a core symptom of PTSD and can make complex trauma symptoms worse because thoughts and feelings are not processed.

2. **True.** The groundbreaking ACE (Adverse Childhood Experiences) study led by Dr. Felitti in 1998 found that adults with more childhood trauma in various categories had greater risk for mental and physical illnesses.

3. **False.** Therapy should be a space where you trust you can bring up any of your concerns.

4. **True.** There are many evidence-based treatments for people who have experienced prolonged childhood trauma according to a meta-analysis across 51 studies by Karatzias et al. in 2019, which compared cognitive behavioral therapy (CBT), exposure alone (EA), and eye movement desensitization and reprocessing (EMDR) to other treatments.

5. **False.** Many nonviolent situations that compromise safety or feel threatening or terrifying can be considered traumas. According to the criteria for PTSD in the (DSM-5), a trauma can be experienced, witnessed, or learned and can include an actual or threatened harm.

What were some of the very real fears and dangers in your life when trauma was happening? How is your life different now in terms of what is present or no longer present?

_____

_____

_____

_____

_____

_____

_____

_____

_____

_____

_____

_____

_____

_____

_____

_____

_____

_____

_____

Have you discussed your traumas? If you have, with whom? What were those conversations like? Who have you not told and why?

What other sources of support have you used to
address your complex trauma? Perhaps you have
sought out therapy, groups, books, or online resources.
How have they helped or not helped?

_____

_____

_____

_____

_____

_____

_____

_____

_____

_____

_____

_____

_____

_____

_____

_____

_____

_____

What progress have you already made in working on your complex trauma? How can you give yourself credit for the work you have already done?

_____

_____

_____

_____

_____

_____

_____

_____

_____

_____

_____

_____

_____

_____

_____

_____

_____

_____

What specific memories or reminders about your trauma come up for you? How often and how intense do they feel? What helps remind you that you are no longer in those situations?

The harm that was done to me or that I witnessed is not my fault or responsibility.

What have you been avoiding that is related to your trauma (for example, activities, feelings, people, places, thoughts)? How would you like this situation to change?

How has fear limited your life? What kinds of experiences do you look forward to having with less fear and anxiety?

_____

_____

_____

_____

_____

_____

_____

_____

_____

_____

_____

_____

_____

_____

_____

_____

_____

_____

How has your view or interpretation of the traumatic events you experienced changed over time if at all? How has your view of healing changed and evolved over time?

What does a good day look like for you? How often in a month do you have a good day? Take some time to reflect on the past week or month and express your gratitude for any of the better days.

List some of your most joyful memories. In some
detail, write down the circumstances, your age, who
was involved, and any other details you'd like to
include. How does thinking about these memories
make you feel?

SELF-MONITORING OF FEELINGS

Any complicated and difficult feelings you may be experiencing are normal when you're working on making a change in your life. Especially when confronting avoidance and dealing with trauma, be aware of and monitor such feelings so that you're more and more equipped to manage them.

What feelings come up as you think about working on your complex trauma symptoms (for example, anger, confusion, fear, or sadness)?

Get creative! Choose your favorite markers, pencils, pens, or crayons and draw a visual representation of what each emotion looks or feels like. Try using different colors, symbols, and images.

Rate each emotion on a scale of 1 to 10 to represent the level of intensity of the feeling, with 1 being the least intense and 10 being the most intense. (We'll revisit your ratings in the next section of the journal, see page 44.)

_____ Anger

_____ Confusion

_____ Fear

_____ Guilt

_____ Hope

_____ Numbness

_____ Sadness

_____ Shame

_____ Other _____

_____ Other _____

_____ Other _____

Write a short letter to your future self describing in detail what you hope for.

_____

_____

_____

_____

_____

_____

_____

_____

_____

_____

_____

_____

_____

_____

_____

_____

_____

_____

_____

_____

_____

Do you see yourself as a victim or a survivor, or does some other word describe your experience better? What do these words mean to you?

_____

_____

_____

_____

_____

_____

_____

_____

_____

_____

_____

_____

_____

_____

_____

_____

_____

_____

_____

_____

Word association: For five minutes, write down words that immediately come to mind when you think of the word "trauma." Then, for five minutes, write down words that immediately come to mind when you think of the word "healing."

PROS AND CONS LIST

Making decisions is not always easy, even when what is beneficial for you may seem clear and obvious. Having some reservations about changing what is familiar to you is normal.

Reflect on the pros and cons of working on your complex post-trauma symptoms and write them in the columns here. What positive outcomes in various areas of your life could come of this work? For example, perhaps you may feel less anxious about relationships or able to enjoy new activities. What changes may not be as positive or could present difficulties? For example, you might have to confront conflict in relationships or deal with fear.

PROS	CONS

Compare the pros and cons lists. Is one longer than the other? Note whether this activity turned out differently than you expected.

_____

_____

_____

_____

Do you have other concerns about your mental health or other diagnoses? Reflect on how these experiences can make trauma recovery more complicated and how working through trauma can have a positive impact on these other concerns.

I will not let fear
or shame block me
from the possibilities of
change in my life.

Freewrite everything that comes to your mind, without edits or judgments, for the next five minutes. Notice what the process is like and what you discover.

_____

_____

_____

_____

_____

_____

_____

_____

_____

_____

_____

_____

_____

_____

_____

_____

_____

_____

I can begin to feel empowered and in control of my life and find meaning in my world.

BASIC DEEP BREATHING

When we are stressed and anxious, a part of our nervous system reacts as a way to prepare our bodies for action. This reaction is known as the "fight-or-flight response" and is an adaptive mechanism that is meant to protect us but can be overwhelming, especially in the absence of a real threat.

Deep, rhythmic breathing allows the calming mechanism of the nervous system to engage. For best effect, engage the diaphragm rather than just pulling in short, shallow breaths from your chest. To practice, either sit or lie down in a comfortable position and place one hand on your chest and another on your belly immediately below your ribs. As you breathe in deeply through your nose and out through your mouth, you should feel the rise of the belly on the inhalation and the fall on the exhalation. Your chest should just barely move.

If you feel comfortable, close your eyes while doing this practice and try to focus on your breath. Do this breathing practice for five minutes at a time at least once a day.

Exploring the Mind-Body Connection

Complex post-traumatic stress disorder consists of clusters of symptoms that impact your thoughts, emotions, and behaviors, and these symptoms interact with one another. Because the body and mind are interconnected, the approach to healing requires addressing both areas.

Our nervous system is our body's primary mechanism for receiving and interpreting messages from our environment. This system, comprising the brain and a network of nerves sending information throughout the body, has adapted to our environment to protect us and allow us to understand experiences. When we feel intense distress or fear associated with trauma, we tend to react with fight, flight, freeze, or submit (acquiescing or feeling helpless) responses. When real danger is present, these reactions of the body are quite effective. The difficulty with complex trauma, however, is that individuals have these intense responses to perceived threat as a learned, self-protective mechanism even when not faced with true danger or threat. Also, the chronic nature of complex trauma means having little opportunity to rebound and recover from traumatic events in safety.

That our nervous system has a built-in calming function, though, is pretty wonderful because we can use it to bring calm and balance to our bodies. We can learn to work with such "threats" as negative thoughts, difficult emotions, and harsh self-talk. Said differently, we can challenge negative thoughts, manage emotions, and engage in self-compassionate behaviors. Healing from trauma is about being more grounded and feeling more in control of your mind-and-body connection. Healing is also about feeling empowered with more options beyond fear responses.

The following prompts, practices, and affirmations will provide guidance. These activities will help you further explore how complex trauma impacts you as a whole person and how different parts of your experience are connected to allow you to become more present. You'll reflect on how your experiences impact your mind and body and use coping skills and interventions to create calm and balance in your thoughts, emotions, and behaviors.

Look back to the practice you did in section 1 entitled, "Goals, Motivation, and Barriers" (see page 6). Reflect and write about the progress you're making toward your goals now that you've learned new skills. How have your levels of motivation changed? What barriers are still challenging? What successes are worthy of celebration?

Look back to the practice in section 1 entitled, "Self-monitoring of Feelings" (see page 26). How have you been managing emotions related to coping with complex trauma? Do the images you drew still represent how you feel? Rerate the intensity of those emotions now that you have learned additional coping skills.

My body, my thoughts, and my emotions empower me to understand and manage how I respond to the world around me.

Think about a time or situation when you felt unsafe. Write down how your body felt and what thoughts and emotions arose. Now think about a time or circumstance during which you truly felt safe. How did you experience your body, mind, and emotions then? How can you re-create these feelings?

Make a fear hierarchy by listing the possible trauma triggers or trauma-related situations or events you tend to avoid. Then rank them from least feared to most feared. Reflect on what making this list was like for you. How you could imagine overcoming these fears?

I am doing the best
I can, and I can learn
new thoughts, behaviors,
and ways to manage
my emotions.

What did you learn about how to feel and express emotions when you were growing up? How did you perceive or experience the ways others in your family managed emotions? To whom did you go when you were feeling distressed as a child?

How do people typically express or talk about emotions in your culture or language? Are there certain emotions that are acceptable and others that seem taboo or off-limits?

_____

_____

_____

_____

_____

_____

_____

_____

_____

_____

_____

_____

_____

_____

_____

_____

_____

When you feel emotions that are difficult to manage, are there any particular indicators that help you notice that these feelings are trauma-related rather than from some other source?

What negative messages have you gotten about your emotional experience or how you express yourself? Think about where these messages came from. How can you challenge what you internalized?

SELF-SOOTHING HAND PRACTICE

This practice allows you to feel grounded and mindfully in touch with your body in the present moment. Choose a location, anywhere you'd like, and take a few minutes or as long feels right to you. You may keep your eyes open or, if you feel comfortable, close them.

Start by taking some deep breaths as you softly, just barely, touch your hands together, making a connection fingertip to fingertip.

Gently and very slowly slide your hands across and around each other as if you're putting on lotion. You might touch your wrists and forearms. Notice sensations you feel, like friction or warmth, sounds you hear, and the rhythmic motion you see or feel.

Continue to apply increasing pressure and speed to this same motion and notice any new sensations.

Keep this feeling of warmth and comfort with you, and use this technique when you need quick self-soothing.

When do you feel most empowered or powerful? What is this feeling like in your body, and what thoughts come along with it? When do you feel most helpless or hopeless? What are your body and mind like in those moments?

What are some thought patterns related to trauma that you want to change? Think about ways you may have learned to think about yourself, others, and the world in such areas as self-esteem, trust, and safety, to name a few examples.

_____

_____

_____

_____

_____

_____

_____

_____

_____

_____

_____

_____

_____

_____

_____

_____

_____

When do you feel most grounded and connected to your body? How does paying attention to your five senses (hearing, sight, smell, taste, and touch) help? You may notice what each of the senses is taking in individually, or you may have one experience where you feel fully aware and connected to your body. How often can you re-create this experience?

Have there been instances during which you felt detached or dissociated from your body, as if you were outside your body or the physical environment around you was not real? What was this experience like? How did you come back to feeling grounded in the present?

My body is mine to nurture,
protect, and enjoy.

Is there a particular emotion you have the most trouble coping with? Imagine and write about what your life would be like if this emotion were less intense or easier to manage.

_____

_____

_____

_____

_____

_____

_____

_____

_____

_____

_____

_____

_____

_____

_____

_____

_____

THREE BOXES PRACTICE

Get into a comfortable position, either lying down or sitting with your feet firmly on the ground. Close your eyes or relax your gaze. Begin to take slow deep breaths, inhaling through your nose for about five seconds and exhaling through your mouth, releasing all the air for about seven seconds. Notice that focusing on your breath alone may be challenging.

Now imagine three boxes: one labeled "emotions," another, "physical sensations," and a third, "thoughts." Note that any of these experiences of self may arise and simply notice the experiences, acknowledging the category of each as they come up. Imagine putting each into its appropriate box. Return your attention to your steady, deep breaths and allow yourself to put distractions away without judgment or analysis. Know that you can process what arises later and, for now, have a moment of peace.

Which of the three boxes was fullest? What was it like to engage in the process of organizing the experiences?

Do you have any chronic physical ailments such as headaches, muscle tension, pain, or other symptoms? Write down your thoughts on how these symptoms may be related to trauma or made more intense by complex trauma symptoms. Distress can have physical impacts on the body. How has trauma impacted your health in general?

With complex trauma and other stigmatized mental health conditions, people tend to compartmentalize or "wear a mask" so that their external behaviors do not match their inner thoughts and feelings. Write about any instances where you may have found yourself in this situation.

MUSIC THERAPY PRACTICE

Think of your four favorite songs that represent or help you cope with the following emotions: anger, fear, joy, and sadness.

Listen to the songs one at a time, fully allowing yourself to become immersed in the sensory experience of hearing the melody and words, feeling the vibrations of the beat, and seeing any visuals associated with the song, like a music video. If the song is slow and rhythmic, notice if your breath syncs with the rhythm of the music. Also allow yourself to experience the way your emotions and physical sensations arise. If you feel comfortable, sing or dance along with the song.

Finally, on the pages that follow, describe or visually represent what your experience was like for each song. What was it like to intentionally use music to experience and cope with your emotions?

Has your trauma created a situation in which you have negative feelings about certain parts of your body or particular aspects of your body? How can you connect with those parts of your body? What aspects of your body do you enjoy or feel positively about?

Sometimes people use defense mechanisms to avoid dealing directly with difficult emotions. You're already likely aware of the purposeful ones, such as distracting yourself or actively suppressing your emotions, but other defense mechanisms may be less conscious, such as projecting feelings onto others. What ways have you tried to avoid or escape your emotions?

What behaviors or survival skills during the time of
the traumatic event(s) you experienced were helpful
at those times but are unhelpful or unnecessary now?
For instance, you may have been constantly on guard
or aggressive.

BEHAVIORAL ACTIVATION

Sometimes complex trauma symptoms can impact daily functioning and healthy behaviors. This situation is especially complicated if you have to continually face reminders or triggers related to the trauma. Adding some structure to your day can help you feel motivated to engage in adaptive behaviors, which allow you to function at your best and have flexibility in the context of stress.

Take some time to create a basic weekly schedule in any form that feels comfortable to you and that would be easiest to use consistently. Examples include a paper calendar, a white board, or an app on your phone. Consider some recurring activities like exercise, leisure time, mealtimes, school, sleep, and work. Notice where you may need to make adjustments to reflect your priorities. Also notice where you may have space for self-care or more enjoyable activities.

Highlight any stressful or triggering events that you may anticipate this week. Think about and write down what coping skills or self-care activities will help you get through these events. What else can you do to mentally prepare to face these situations?

Continue to revisit these questions and decide on the best method to keep your schedule, whether digital or on paper.

I can be fully present
and engaged in my life.

When you encounter a crisis or a trauma trigger, does your response tend to be fight (aggression), flight (escape), freeze (become numb or detached), or submit (acquiesce or feel powerless)? Have your responses become stronger or weaker over time?

I can shift my perspective
toward gratitude and hope.

THOUGHT RECORD PRACTICE

When you notice a shift in your mood, use the table on the next two pages to write down the details of your experience. Doing so will help you understand how your thoughts, feelings, and behaviors are connected. You can also determine whether there is a particular pattern in your responses to particular triggers, which will help you practice coping with distressing thoughts and feelings. You'll find an example to help you get started.

PART ONE

EMOTION (INTENSITY 0–100)	WHAT TRIGGERED THE SHIFT IN EMOTION?	THOUGHTS ASSOCIATED TO THE TRIGGER AND EMOTION
Anger—80	Friend made a comment making light of my trauma experience. They asked why I didn't just leave the violent relationship.	My friend thinks I'm weak and stupid. Maybe it was my fault.

PART TWO

EVIDENCE FOR THOUGHTS	REFRAME OR CHALLENGE YOUR THOUGHTS BY THINKING OF ALTERNATIVES	EMOTION AFTER REFLECTION (INTENSITY 0-100)
There have been a couple other times my friend made inappropriate comments. I could have left the first time it happened.	My friend and I have had many positive interactions where they have praised me. Maybe they did not have malicious intentions. The abuse I endured happened because my partner hurt me and not because of anything I did. Leaving was really hard.	Anger—25

To what extent do you feel in control of your thoughts, emotions, and behaviors? What do you imagine your life would look like if you felt even more in control of managing these experiences?

Cultivating a Healthy Sense of Self

Complex PTSD develops after chronic, prolonged traumatic events or circumstances of abuse, neglect, violence, or threats of violence. Many of these events are interpersonal, meaning they are caused or influenced by another person and, thus, impact the way an individual sees themselves, others, and the world in general. Particularly when chronic childhood traumas occur, there's a tremendous impact on how someone sees themselves and how they build relationships with others.

The traumas can affect a person's capacity for healthy attachment, their ability to trust, how they set boundaries between self and others, and their self-esteem.

Healing from chronic post-traumatic stress disorder in the interpersonal realm is about realizing that the harm done to you was not your fault. A violation of your boundaries and safety is not something you or anyone deserves. You are a person deserving of safety, self-compassion, care, balance, and joy in your life as well as compassion and healthy relationships with others. Healing from trauma symptoms will mean becoming increasingly in touch with how you feel, what you need and desire, and how you can fulfill those needs in healthy ways, as well as noticing how you manage distress.

Often trauma results in feeling like the different parts of your life are compartmentalized or that you are not very solid in your identity. Shifting the way you relate to yourself and others can allow opportunities to be curious and reflective, to love yourself, and to reengage with trusting and loving relationships with others. This endeavor is holistic—encompassing physical, psychological, and spiritual needs. In this section, you'll be prompted to write in a self-reflective manner, to do practices that may challenge you, and to affirm your unique sense of self.

These activities will help you generate insight and self-compassion. Self-compassion and kind regard for yourself will create a better foundation for consistent self-care. As you practice reflections and interventions aimed at your continued learning and appreciation of yourself, you can better assess your needs, desires, values, and relationship boundaries.

Look back to the prompt in section 1, where you were asked to tell someone about your journey (see page 10). How have you kept yourself accountable in your healing journey? How has this trusted person helped along the way? Think about revisiting this conversation and sharing your progress with this trusted person.

Look back to the prompt in section 1 about a letter to your future self (see page 29). How likely do you think it is that your hopes and desires for yourself will be fulfilled? How can you make these hopes and desires happen?

Look back to the prompt in section 2: "What did you learn about how to feel and express emotions when you were growing up?" (see page 49). What aspects of your early learning about emotions would you like to unlearn or change?

When do you feel most authentic and in tune with yourself? When in a specific place? Doing a specific activity? Or in other contexts?

Write down the first 10 words you would use to describe yourself. Now write down 10 more you would like to be applied to you. How close are you to feeling that the aspirational descriptions fit?

SELF-CARE CHECKLIST

Rate on a scale of 1 to 5 how often you engage in these self-care activities, with 1 being never and 5 being almost always. Afterward, if you'd like, reflect on what you are doing really well and where you might improve.

BEHAVIORAL

____ Arranging your home or workspace to be comfortable

____ Asking for help when needed

____ Planning and organizing to complete important tasks

____ Setting realistic goals

____ Taking breaks from work- or school-related tasks

EMOTIONAL

____ Allowing yourself to cry and express difficult feelings

____ Finding what helps you experience joy and laughter

____ Giving yourself affirmations

____ Identifying what brings you comfort

____ Spending time with others you enjoy

PHYSICAL

____ Eating healthy foods regularly

____ Exercising

____ Getting enough sleep

____ Getting regular medical care

____ Monitoring your sexual health

PSYCHOLOGICAL

____ Being vulnerable with others

____ Engaging your mind in other areas or hobbies
beyond work

____ Going to therapy

____ Self-reflecting

____ Setting healthy boundaries

OTHER

_____

_____

_____

What are the power dynamics in your relationships? Reflect and describe whether you tend to have less, equal, or more power in relationships. How do these power balances or imbalances impact you?

Would you describe yourself as passive, assertive, or aggressive? How has your trauma experience impacted your interpersonal stance? How would you like your place in relationships to change to achieve better balance?

I have the right to fully
and authentically feel and
express my feelings.

Who is the person you are closest to? Write down some characteristics about or experiences with this person that have allowed you to trust them.

What kinds of relationship patterns—between your parents, yourself and your parents, yourself and teachers, yourself and other adults, or yourself and other children—did you see or experience in your life when you were a child? How has what you saw influenced how you relate to others?

I have all of the resources
I need within me to cope
with my trauma and to ask
for help when I need it.

What are 15 things you can be grateful for today?
Reflect on what making this list is like.

1. _____

2. _____

3. _____

4. _____

5. _____

6. _____

7. _____

8. _____

9. _____

10. _____

11. _____

12. _____

13. _____

14. _____

15. _____

I am doing the best I can.

What are some factors that have gotten in the way of your ability to practice self-compassion and self-care regularly? What factors help facilitate these practices?

PERSONAL NEEDS ASSESSMENT

Check in with yourself by doing a personal needs assessment. Ask yourself the following questions to reflect on needs and potential solutions to those needs:

■ How am I feeling generally today (emotionally and physically)?

■ What seems missing, or what activity would make me feel more balanced if it were added to my day?

■ What resources (tangible or intangible) do I have to meet these needs?

■ How will I feel when these needs are met?

The answers to these questions could lead to realizations that, for example, getting more sleep could help you feel more energized, reaching out to a friend could help you feel less alone, or eating a better breakfast may help you feel less irritable.

Set a timer for five minutes and write down every
enjoyable activity you can think of. Put a star by the
ones you would like to do more often and make a plan
this week to do at least one.

MINDFUL EATING

We typically do many daily activities, for example, eating, without awareness and involvement in the present experience, in a way that is not mindful. Putting your focus on eating and other basic activities can bring groundedness and awareness of the present that help manage experiences and emotions as they come.

Pick a food you enjoy that has complex flavors or textures. You can try this practice with one bite or one piece and work up to eating a full meal more mindfully.

Follow the steps below to use all your senses to experience the food:

1. Look at the food and notice the colors, textures, shapes, and sizes.

2. Notice the smell of the food, slowly taking in deep breaths.

3. Notice the texture of the food as you touch it with your hands or a utensil.

4. Take a bite of the food and chew slowly and mindfully.

5. Notice the taste and any sounds you make as you chew.

6. Pay attention to how you feel as you eat the food.

How much of your view of yourself is through a trauma-related lens? Do you primarily think of yourself as a traumatized person or a person with C-PTSD? Reflect on these questions. Later, list as many other positive characteristics or strengths you have apart from surviving trauma.

Have other people in your family experienced the same or similar traumas? Were other people present with you when the traumatic events happened (for example, siblings)? How is this situation discussed in your family or across generations?

_____

_____

_____

_____

_____

_____

_____

_____

_____

_____

_____

_____

_____

_____

_____

_____

_____

_____

Draw pictures, use symbols, or list words that describe your past, present, and future ideas of yourself. How are they similar or different?

DREAM JOURNAL

The next time you have a dream and can remember what you dreamt in some detail, begin a journal, answering the following questions to interpret the dream:

- What happened in the dream? Who/what/when/where/how?

- Were there any particular themes or symbols in the dream that have meaning for you?

- What emotions did you feel in the dream and how did you feel upon waking?

- Why do you think you are having this dream now? What was going on in your life on this day or in the recent past?

- Is the dream related to your traumas? If so, how?

Is there anyone in your life you know or even someone in the public eye who you consider to be a role model specifically for managing mental health or trauma? What practices of theirs could you borrow for yourself? If you're close to them, what would reaching out to them be like for you?

I am worthy and deserving of care, kindness, love, and respect.

Think of someone for whom you feel immense love
and compassion and write down 10 to 15 positive
thoughts or wishes for them. Now turn and say these
things to yourself. How does saying these words feel?
Do you believe you are a person worthy of kindness
and compassion?

I have the right to set whatever boundaries make me feel safe and to ask that others respect those boundaries.

When you think of yourself, what age do you feel like you are regardless of your actual age? Has your trauma impacted your perception of your age? If so, how? (Sometimes, people who have experienced trauma can feel stuck in a certain period of their lives.)

What does self-love mean to you? Write about how you
have or have not expressed self-love.

_____

_____

_____

_____

_____

_____

_____

_____

_____

_____

_____

_____

_____

_____

_____

_____

_____

_____

A LOVING-KINDNESS MEDITATION
FOR SELF-COMPASSION

Start by sitting or lying down in a comfortable position and resting or closing your eyes.

1. Take some deep breaths, inhaling through the nose for about five seconds and breathing out through the mouth for about seven seconds, releasing all the air in your body as well as any tension you're carrying.

2. As you become more and more relaxed, direct compassion toward yourself as you repeat in your mind or aloud, "May I be well, may I be happy, may I be safe."

3. Now think of someone you love and feel close to. You may focus on someone whose image brings comfort to you and direct compassion toward them repeating, "May they be well, may they be happy, may they be safe."

4. Challenge yourself to think of someone you are not close to or even someone with whom you have had conflict. Send compassion their way by repeating, "May they be well, may they be happy, may they be safe."

5. Finally to all living things, say: "May they be well, may they be happy, may they be safe."

How does feeling or not feeling self-love impact your
relationships with others?

_____

_____

_____

_____

_____

_____

_____

_____

_____

_____

_____

_____

_____

_____

_____

_____

_____

_____

_____

SECTION 4

Continuing Your Healing Journey

At this point, hopefully you are closer to a place where you feel more confident about how to manage your trauma symptoms. Especially if you've followed the journal in order, you've worked through the beginning stages of learning to heal. Recovering from complex trauma is a long process of learning, healing, and adjusting. Your symptoms may not be completely resolved.

Of course, with the ongoing support of others, including professionals, and with the skills you've learned, you are equipped to continue this work toward a healthier balance in your life.

Be reminded that trauma is a *part* of your life and not the whole story of your life or who you are as a person. Complex trauma responses are complicated reactions to extreme circumstances of harm that should not have happened. As you continue this process, there are opportunities for you to make meaning of your life's experiences and grow to become even more resilient.

Everyone, including you, is deserving of safety and care. Do not hesitate to reach out to trusted people in your life to provide that support and to continue to learn and practice skills to provide care and compassion to yourself. When you encounter a setback, which is normal and very likely to happen, do not forget the progress you have made up to that point. Feel free to continue to come back to the pages of this journal for review. You can keep moving forward toward a balanced and healthy life in the future.

This final set of activities will allow you to review and consolidate your experiences as you look toward the future. Also, looking at the progress you have made up to this point can be a great motivator to keep going.

Consider again the first affirmation in section 1 of this journal: "I have many personal strengths that will allow me to achieve my goals" (see page 4). Has reciting this or other affirmations throughout felt easier and more authentic as you've worked through the journal? If not, what gets in the way?

Look back to the prompt in section 3 about enjoyable activities (see page 98). What enjoyable activities have you continued to do and which ones would you still like to do more often?

Look back to your "Self-care Checklist" in section 3 (see page 86). Re-rate the frequency at which you're doing self-care activities. Have you improved? If so, how?

What is the most valuable lesson you've learned about yourself, others, or the world after having experienced your trauma?

_____

_____

_____

_____

_____

_____

_____

_____

_____

_____

_____

_____

_____

_____

_____

_____

_____

_____

VALUES SORTING

Part 1. Take a look at the list of values in the table below. You may also think of additional values and add them to the word bank. Then place each value from the word bank in the appropriate column related to level of importance in the table on page 120.

VALUES WORD BANK		
Ambition	Curiosity	Peace
Autonomy	Growth	Power
Change	Honesty	Solitude
Community	Intelligence	Spirituality
Compassion	Intimacy	Wealth

VERY IMPORTANT TO ME	IMPORTANT TO ME	NOT IMPORTANT TO ME

Part 2. Now reflect on how completing this process was for you. Then, for the values you categorized as "very important to me," ask yourself the following questions: How am I living up to honoring those values and what might I do differently? What will my life be like when I am fully honoring the values that are important?

What are you hopeful about or looking forward
to in your future after having worked on your
complex trauma?

_____

_____

_____

_____

_____

_____

_____

_____

_____

_____

_____

_____

_____

_____

_____

_____

_____

_____

_____

What has been the most challenging aspect of intentionally confronting your trauma and doing the work to recover? Write about whether the process was easier or more difficult than you anticipated and how you got through any challenges.

I have overcome
many obstacles in my
life, and I can continue
to look forward to the
future with hope.

Are there any aspects of your trauma stories or complex trauma symptoms you find especially difficult to let go of? Reflect on what may be the source of this difficulty.

_____

_____

_____

_____

_____

_____

_____

_____

_____

_____

_____

_____

_____

_____

_____

_____

_____

MINDFULNESS MEDITATION ON GOALS

1. Begin by finding a comfortable position, sitting or lying down.

2. Gently close your eyes or rest your gaze. Begin to take slow, deep breaths in through your nose, filling your lungs with air, and out through your mouth, releasing all the air and tension in your body. If thoughts or distractions come up, allow them to come and pass without judgment and then return your focus to your breath.

3. As you continue to take deep breaths, repeat the following phrases either aloud or silently in your mind:

   May I have success in accomplishing the goals I set.
   May barriers be minimal and temporary.
   May I celebrate my achievements and growth.

4. After 5 to 10 minutes, gently begin to focus your attention again on the sensations around you and allow yourself to return to the present.

Write down what you have come to know as patterns of trauma reactions you experience. How will you replace those patterns with healthy coping behaviors from now on? For example, if you typically avoid any sign of conflict, you may replace that avoidance with assertive communication.

How do you imagine your relationships with others will change as you continue to heal and grow from complex trauma?

_____

_____

_____

_____

_____

_____

_____

_____

_____

_____

_____

_____

_____

_____

_____

_____

_____

_____

How do you imagine you will manage new stressors or difficulties that arise in your life? Write about how prepared and equipped you feel to manage emotions.

Have you become more open to talking about your experiences or seeking support from others (or both)? If so, what is that experience like? If not, what barriers may still be in the way?

May my life be filled with
growth, love, strength,
and support.

What new personal strengths have you learned about yourself as you reflect on the process of working on complex trauma? Are there strengths you knew you had before that have reemerged?

REVIEW OF PROGRESS

You have come so far on this journey and likely have made progress and changes compared to where you started when you picked up this journal. Acknowledging your progress is important, not only to give yourself credit but to guide you toward what is next.

Look back to the practice in section 1 entitled, "Goals, Motivation, and Barriers" (see page 6) to revisit the goals you set in this journal. For each goal, rate the level of progress you've made on a scale from 0 to 100, with 0 being no progress at all and 100 being achievement of your goal.

Next, write down any remaining barriers you have to achieving these goals and what actions you may take to keep moving forward. The first one is done for you as an example.

Goal: Decrease anxiety about riding on trains where the assault happened.

My progress: 75—I can get on the train at that station during the daytime and if there are other people around; I feel safer than I used to.

Remaining barriers: I want to be able to ride the train at any time I need to. I didn't see the face of the person who assaulted me so I won't know if they are around again.

Actions: Practice breathing exercises before and during traveling to self-soothe, create a safety plan for crises, and continue to remind myself I am in the present.

Goal: _____

My Progress: _____

_____

Remaining Barriers: _____

_____

Actions: _____

_____

Goal: _____

My Progress: _____

_____

Remaining Barriers: _____

_____

Actions: _____

_____

Goal: _____

My Progress: _____

_____

Remaining Barriers: _____

_____

Actions: _____

_____

Goal: _____

My Progress: _____

_____

Remaining Barriers: _____

_____

Actions: _____

_____

Plan an enjoyable activity or reward to congratulate yourself.

What does resilience mean to you? Write down several examples of how you have exhibited resilience. If you have trouble bringing any to mind, write down examples of how you would like to exhibit resilience when challenges arise.

Resilience is a capacity that can generalize to many other areas of your life beyond coping with trauma and triggers. In what other areas of your life do you think your increased resilience will help you achieve goals? These may be areas such as interpersonal relationships, school, or work.

I am ready to embrace
new challenges that
arise with strength
and compassion.

How have others noticed any changes in you since you've begun this journey? Write about what hearing observations and feedback from other people in your life is like for you.

Are there any ways in which you view yourself differently after having started this work?

_____

_____

_____

_____

_____

_____

_____

_____

_____

_____

_____

_____

_____

_____

_____

_____

_____

_____

_____

I am learning to love
the person I am growing
to be each day.

Often, people who have experienced chronic trauma can experience a great deal of shame, self-blame, fear, and confusion surrounding particular trauma memories. Write about any ways in which you view your trauma memories differently now since beginning this process.

GUIDED IMAGERY—SAFE PLACE

1. Start by finding a comfortable place where you can sit or lie down.

2. Gently close your eyes or rest your gaze.

3. Begin to take slow, deep breaths in through your nose, filling your lungs with air, and out through your mouth, releasing all the air and tension in your body. If thoughts or distractions come up, allow them to come and pass without judgment, and return your focus to your breath.

4. When you feel settled, begin to imagine with all your senses a place where you can picture feeling safe. This place can be real or imagined, past or present. Carefully envision in as much detail as possible what you can see around you, what you hear, and what you can touch, smell, and taste.

5. Imagine a sense of peace and safety coming over you as you rest or explore this place.

6. Continue taking deep breaths. After 5 to 10 minutes, start to bring your attention back to the present, knowing that you can always revisit this place.

How will this journal continue to fit into your growth and healing from complex trauma? You're encouraged to revisit what you've written and to practice the activities and skills you've learned.

Peruse the resource section of this journal (see page 153). Write down what particular resources would be specifically helpful to you, why they would be most helpful, and how you might engage in utilizing them.

SAFETY PLAN

Equipped with all of the tools you've practiced so far, create a safety plan for various situations of crisis or intense emotional distress. Having a plan in place can provide structure and be critical when managing overwhelming situations.

If I begin to make a plan to harm or kill myself, I can:

Call 911 or go to my local emergency room.

_____

_____

_____

_____

_____

If I have thoughts of self-harm or suicide but haven't formulated a plan on how to carry out these thoughts, I can:

Contact my therapist or other source of support.

_____

_____

_____

_____

_____

If I experienced complex trauma symptoms or triggers, I can:

Practice a mindfulness exercise such as guided imagery, imagining a safer place.

I can use these coping skills when I feel:

Sad

Angry

Anxious

_____

_____

_____

Guilty

_____

_____

_____

Numb

_____

_____

_____

Ashamed

_____

_____

_____

I can identify safe and supportive people in my life to whom I can reach out for help and support. I do not have to heal alone.

Write down, in any words that feel fitting, your commitment to continue your healing journey and how you will fulfill that commitment.

_____

_____

_____

_____

_____

_____

_____

_____

_____

_____

_____

_____

_____

_____

_____

_____

_____

Resources

Emergency Resources

National Suicide Prevention Lifeline 1-800-273-8225

Call 911 or go to your nearest psychiatric emergency room.

Trauma and Self-care Online Resources

American Psychiatric Association page on PTSD provides information for patients and families, and additional resources to find help, apa.org/topics/ptsd.

Complextrauma.org is a site that provides books, articles, videos, and other resources specifically for complex trauma, complextrauma.org.

The CPTSD Foundation offers a book club, support groups, and other online resources for recovery support, cptsdfoundation .org/cptsd-resources.

Mindful.org is a great resource for mindfulness and meditation activities, mindful.org.

The National Child Traumatic Stress Network provides literature, videos, and resources related to childhood trauma. These resources can also be helpful for adult survivors of childhood trauma to gain insight, nctsn.org/what-is-child-trauma/trauma-types/complex-trauma.

The PTSD Alliance provides information on PTSD and resources to get help, ptsdalliance.org.

RAINN is the Rape, Abuse, & Incest National Network. This resource is specifically geared toward survivors of sexual trauma and includes a hotline, research on sexual violence, survivor stories, legal information, and news, rainn.org.

Popular Books on Trauma and Complex Trauma

Adult Children of Emotionally Immature Parents by Lindsay C. Gibson explores the impact of early attachment and parenting.

The Body Keeps the Score by Bessel van der Kolk is a thorough exploration of how trauma impacts the mind and body, and what interventions can impact healing. The book includes both clinical information and narratives of trauma treatment.

Complex PTSD: From Surviving to Thriving by Pete Walker is a practical self-help guide to recover from complex trauma.

The Drama of the Gifted Child by Alice Miller explores the lasting impacts of childhood trauma.

Therapist Directories

General resources to find a therapist near you in person or working virtually across a range of areas of specialization:

Good Therapy: goodtherapy.org

Psychology Today: psychologytoday.com

Therapy directories specifically for people of color, lower-income, LGBTQIA+, and other marginalized communities:

Latinx Therapy: latinxtherapy.com

Lighthouse LGBTQ Affirming Directory: lighthouse.lgbt

Open Path Psychotherapy Collective: openpathcollective.org

Therapy for Black Girls: therapyforblackgirls.com

References

American Psychiatric Association. *Diagnostic and Statistical Manual of Mental Disorders: DSM-5*. Arlington, VA: American Psychiatric Association, 2013.

Badour, Christal L., Daniel M. Blonigen, Matthew Tyler Boden, Matthew T. Feldner, and Marcel O. Bonn-Miller. "A Longitudinal Test of the Bi-Directional Relations Between Avoidance Coping and PTSD Severity During and After PTSD Treatment." *Behaviour Research and Therapy* 50, no. 10 (2012): 610–616.

Cloitre, Marylene, Bradley C. Stolbach, Judith L. Herman, Bessel van der Kolk, Robert Pynoos, Jing Wang, and Eva Petkova. "A Developmental Approach to Complex PTSD: Childhood and Adult Cumulative Trauma as Predictors of Symptom Complexity." *Journal of Traumatic Stress* 22, no. 5 (2009): 399–408.

Cloitre, Marylene, Lisa R. Cohen, Kile M. Ortigo, Christie Jackson, and Karestan C. Koenen. *Treating Survivors of Childhood Abuse and Interpersonal Trauma: STAIR Narrative Therapy*. New York: Guilford Publications, 2020.

Felitti, Vincent J., Robert F. Anda, Dale Nordenberg, David F.
  Williamson, Alison M. Spitz, Valerie Edwards, and James
  S. Marks. "Relationship of Childhood Abuse and House-
  hold Dysfunction to Many of the Leading Causes of Death
  in Adults: The Adverse Childhood Experiences (ACE)
  Study." *American Journal of Preventive Medicine* 14, no. 4
  (1998): 245–258.

Herman, Judith Lewis. "Complex PTSD: A Syndrome in
  Survivors of Prolonged and Repeated Trauma." *Journal of
  Traumatic Stress* 5, no. 3 (1992): 377–391.

Karatzias, Thanos, Philip Murphy, Marylene Cloitre, Jonathan
  Bisson, Neil Roberts, Mark Shevlin, Philip Hyland et al.
  "Psychological Interventions for ICD-11 Complex PTSD
  Symptoms: Systematic Review and Meta-analysis."
  Psychological Medicine 49, no. 11 (2019): 1761–1775.

Maercker, Andreas, Chris R. Brewin, Richard A. Bryant,
  Marylene Cloitre, Mark van Ommeren, Lynne M. Jones,
  Asma Humayan et al. "Diagnosis and Classification of
  Disorders Specifically Associated with Stress: Proposals for
  ICD-11." *World Psychiatry* 12, no. 3 (2013): 198–206.

Shenk, Chad E., Frank W. Putnam, and Jennie G. Noll. "Experiential Avoidance and the Relationship Between Child Maltreatment and PTSD Symptoms: Preliminary Evidence." *Child Abuse & Neglect* 36, no. 2 (2012): 118–126.

World Health Organization. *International Classification of Diseases for Mortality and Morbidity Statistics*, 11th edition. Geneva: World Health Organization, 2018.